THIS CRUISE JOURNAL BELONGS TO:

_____

CRUISE BUCKET LIST

PLACES I WANT TO VISIT:

_____
_____
_____
_____
_____
_____
_____
_____
_____
_____

THINGS I WANT TO SEE:

_____
_____
_____
_____
_____
_____
_____
_____
_____
_____
_____
_____

TOP 3 DESTINATIONS:

_____
_____
_____

CRUISE SAVINGS

WE'RE SAVING FOR: _____

AMOUNT NEEDED: _____

OUR GOAL DATE:

$

DEPOSIT TRACKER

AMOUNT DEPOSITED: **DATE DEPOSITED:**

$ _____   _____

$ _____   _____

$ _____   _____

$ _____   _____

$ _____   _____

$ _____   _____

$ _____   _____

$ _____   _____

$ _____   _____

$ _____   _____

CRUISE SAVINGS

DEPOSIT TRACKER

AMOUNT DEPOSITED: **DATE DEPOSITED:**

$ _____   _____

$ _____   _____

$ _____   _____

$ _____   _____

$ _____   _____

$ _____   _____

$ _____   _____

$ _____   _____

$ _____   _____

$ _____   _____

$ _____   _____

$ _____   _____

$ _____   _____

ALL ABOARD!

PRE-CRUISE TO DO LIST & CHECKLIST

1 MONTH BEFORE

2 WEEKS BEFORE

1 WEEK BEFORE

2 DAYS BEFORE

24 HOURS BEFORE

DAY OF TRAVEL

FLIGHT INFORMATION

DATE: _____   DESTINATION: _____

AIRLINE:	
BOOKING NUMBER:	
DEPARTURE DATE:	
BOARDING TIME	
GATE NUMBER:	
SEAT NUMBER	
ARRIVAL / LANDING TIME:	

DATE: _____   DESTINATION: _____

AIRLINE:	
BOOKING NUMBER:	
DEPARTURE DATE:	
BOARDING TIME:	
GATE NUMBER:	
SEAT NUMBER:	
ARRIVAL / LANDING TIME:	

CRUISE PACKING CHECKLIST

CLOTHING	✓	ESSENTIALS	✓

CRUISE PACKING CHECKLIST

CLOTHING FOR HER	✓	CLOTHING FOR HIM	✓

ESSENTIALS	✓	FOR THE JOURNEY	✓
		IMPORTANT DOCUMENTS	✓

SAMPLE CRUISE PACKING CHECKLIST

CLOTHING FOR HER	✓	CLOTHING FOR HIM	✓
T-Shirts &, Tank Tops & Blouses		T-Shirts & Tank Tops	
Sundresses		Shorts	
Flip Flops, Sandals & Heels		Swim Wear	
Shorts & Pants		Jeans, Khakis	
Swimsuit & Cover Up		Formal Attire (dress shirt, shoes, etc.)	
T-Shirts &, Tank Tops & Blouses		Belt	
Aqua/Swimming Shoes		Tie	
Bras, Panties & Socks		Sandals / Sneakers	
Sunhat		Visor, Baseball Cap	
Sunglasses		T-Shirts &, Tank Tops & Blouses	
Formal Attire		Sunglasses	
Jewelry		Socks & Underwear	

ESSENTIALS	✓	FOR THE JOURNEY	✓
Lanyard		Carry On Bag	
Suntan Lotion		Cash / Local Currency	
Medication (motion sickness, etc.)		Credit Cards	
Travel Mug / Water Bottle		Phone Charger	
		Backpack	

		IMPORTANT DOCUMENTS	✓
		Passport & ID	
		Cruise Documents & Boarding Pass	
		Flight Information	

CRUISE ITINERARY

Monday

Tuesday

Wednesday

Thursday

Friday

Saturday

Sunday

CRUISE DETAILS

NOTES

TO DO:

CRUISE DETAILS & REMINDERS:

CRUISING TO DO LIST

CRUISE EXCURSION PLANNER

ACTIVITY / EXCURSION OVERVIEW:

EST COST OF EXCURSION:

INCLUSIONS:	✓	**EXCLUSIONS:**	✓
FOOD & DRINK:	☐		☐
TRANSPORTATION:	☐		☐
GRATUITY:	☐		☐

ACTUAL COST:

IMPORTANT INFORMATION:

CONTACT: _____ PHONE #: _____

MEET UP TIME: _____ WHAT TO BRING: _____

ADDRESS: _____

CRUISE EXCURSION PLANNER

ACTIVITY / EXCURSION OVERVIEW:

EST COST OF EXCURSION:

INCLUSIONS:	✓	**EXCLUSIONS:**	✓
FOOD & DRINK:	☐		☐
TRANSPORTATION:	☐		☐
GRATUITY:	☐		☐

ACTUAL COST:

IMPORTANT INFORMATION:

CONTACT: _____ PHONE #: _____

MEET UP TIME: _____ WHAT TO BRING: _____

ADDRESS: _____

CRUISE EXCURSION PLANNER

ACTIVITY / EXCURSION OVERVIEW:

EST COST OF EXCURSION:

INCLUSIONS:	✓	**EXCLUSIONS:**	✓
FOOD & DRINK:	☐		☐
TRANSPORTATION:	☐		☐
GRATUITY:	☐		☐

ACTUAL COST:

IMPORTANT INFORMATION:

CONTACT: _____ PHONE #: _____

MEET UP TIME: _____ WHAT TO BRING: _____

ADDRESS: _____

CRUISE EXCURSION PLANNER

ACTIVITY / EXCURSION OVERVIEW:

EST COST OF EXCURSION:

INCLUSIONS:	✓	**EXCLUSIONS:**	✓
FOOD & DRINK:	☐		☐
TRANSPORTATION:	☐		☐
GRATUITY:	☐		☐

ACTUAL COST:

IMPORTANT INFORMATION:

CONTACT: _____ PHONE #: _____

MEET UP TIME: _____ WHAT TO BRING: _____

ADDRESS: _____

CRUISE PORT PLANNER

DESTINATION: DATE:

THINGS TO DO / SEE:

WHERE TO EAT:

TRANSPORTATION DETAILS:

OTHER INFORMATION:

RETURN TO SHIP BY:

CRUISE PORT PLANNER

DESTINATION: DATE:

THINGS TO DO / SEE:

WHERE TO EAT:

TRANSPORTATION DETAILS:

OTHER INFORMATION:

RETURN TO SHIP BY:

CRUISE PORT PLANNER

DESTINATION: DATE:

THINGS TO DO / SEE:

☐
☐
☐
☐
☐
☐
☐

WHERE TO EAT:

☐
☐
☐
☐
☐
☐
☐

TRANSPORTATION DETAILS:

☐
☐
☐
☐
☐

OTHER INFORMATION:

☐
☐
☐
☐
☐

RETURN TO SHIP BY:

CRUISE PORT PLANNER

DESTINATION: | DATE:

THINGS TO DO / SEE:

WHERE TO EAT:

TRANSPORTATION DETAILS:

OTHER INFORMATION:

RETURN TO SHIP BY:

CRUISE PORT PLANNER

DESTINATION: DATE:

THINGS TO DO / SEE:

WHERE TO EAT:

TRANSPORTATION DETAILS:

OTHER INFORMATION:

RETURN TO SHIP BY:

CRUISE PLANNER

WEEK OF:

MONDAY	TUESDAY	WEDNESDAY	THURSDAY
TO DO	TO DO	TO DO	TO DO
MEALS	MEALS	MEALS	MEALS

FRIDAY	SATURDAY	SUNDAY	NOTES
TO DO	TO DO	TO DO	
MEALS	MEALS	MEALS	MEALS

CRUISE ACTIVITIES

ACTIVITY PLANNER:

	M	T	W	T	F	S	S
	○	○	○	○	○	○	○
	○	○	○	○	○	○	○
	○	○	○	○	○	○	○
	○	○	○	○	○	○	○
	○	○	○	○	○	○	○
	○	○	○	○	○	○	○
	○	○	○	○	○	○	○
	○	○	○	○	○	○	○
	○	○	○	○	○	○	○
	○	○	○	○	○	○	○
	○	○	○	○	○	○	○
	○	○	○	○	○	○	○
	○	○	○	○	○	○	○
	○	○	○	○	○	○	○

DAILY ACTIVITY PLANNER

DAILY ITINERARY

ACTIVITY: ....

TIME: ....

LOCATION: ....

WEATHER:

MEAL PLANNER

DAILY EXPENSES

TOTAL COST:

TOP ACTIVITIES

TIME:	SCHEDULE:

NOTES:

DAILY ACTIVITY PLANNER

DAILY ITINERARY

ACTIVITY: ....

TIME: ....

LOCATION: ....

WEATHER:

TOP ACTIVITIES

MEAL PLANNER

TIME:	SCHEDULE:

DAILY EXPENSES

TOTAL COST:

NOTES:

DAILY ACTIVITY PLANNER

DAILY ITINERARY

ACTIVITY: _____

TIME: _____

LOCATION: _____

WEATHER: ☀ ⛅ 🌦 ☁ ⛈

MEAL PLANNER

DAILY EXPENSES

_____   _____

_____   _____

_____   _____

_____   _____

TOTAL COST: [   ]

TOP ACTIVITIES

TIME:	SCHEDULE:

NOTES:

DAILY ACTIVITY PLANNER

DAILY ITINERARY

ACTIVITY: _____

TIME: _____

LOCATION: _____

WEATHER:

MEAL PLANNER

DAILY EXPENSES

_____   _____

_____   _____

_____   _____

_____   _____

TOTAL COST: [   ]

TOP ACTIVITIES

TIME:	SCHEDULE:

NOTES:

DAILY ACTIVITY PLANNER

DAILY ITINERARY

ACTIVITY:

TIME:

LOCATION:

WEATHER:

MEAL PLANNER

DAILY EXPENSES

TOTAL COST:

TOP ACTIVITIES

TIME:	SCHEDULE:

NOTES:

DAILY ACTIVITY PLANNER

DAILY ITINERARY

ACTIVITY: ....

TIME: ....

LOCATION: ....

WEATHER: ☀ ⛅ 🌦 ☁ ⛈

MEAL PLANNER

DAILY EXPENSES

TOTAL COST:

TOP ACTIVITIES

TIME: SCHEDULE:

NOTES:

DAILY ACTIVITY PLANNER

DAILY ITINERARY

ACTIVITY: ....

TIME: ....

LOCATION: ....

WEATHER: ☀ ⛅ 🌦 ☁ ⛈

MEAL PLANNER

TOP ACTIVITIES

TIME:	SCHEDULE:

DAILY EXPENSES

TOTAL COST: [   ]

NOTES:

MY CRUISE JOURNAL

DATE:

What I Did Today:

Highlight of the Day:

Thoughts & Reflections:

MY CRUISE JOURNAL

DATE:

What I Did Today:

Highlight of the Day:

Thoughts & Reflections:

MY CRUISE JOURNAL

DATE:

What I Did Today:

Highlight of the Day:

Thoughts & Reflections:

MY CRUISE JOURNAL

DATE:

What I Did Today:

Highlight of the Day:

Thoughts & Reflections:

MY CRUISE JOURNAL

DATE:

What I Did Today:

Highlight of the Day:

Thoughts & Reflections:

MY CRUISE JOURNAL

DATE:

What I Did Today:

Highlight of the Day:

Thoughts & Reflections:

MY CRUISE JOURNAL

DATE:

What I Did Today:

Highlight of the Day:

Thoughts & Reflections:

CRUISE FRIENDS

FRIENDS ARE FOREVER

NAME:

PHONE NUMBER:

ADDRESS:

CABIN #:

FRIENDS ARE FOREVER

NAME:

PHONE NUMBER:

ADDRESS:

CABIN #:

FRIENDS ARE FOREVER

NAME:

PHONE NUMBER:

ADDRESS:

CABIN #:

FRIENDS ARE FOREVER

NAME:

PHONE NUMBER:

ADDRESS:

CABIN #:

There's Nothing Like Cruising Life!

CRUISE SAVINGS

WE'RE SAVING FOR: _____

AMOUNT NEEDED: _____

OUR GOAL DATE: _____

$

DEPOSIT TRACKER

AMOUNT DEPOSITED: **DATE DEPOSITED:**

$ _____   _____

$ _____   _____

$ _____   _____

$ _____   _____

$ _____   _____

$ _____   _____

$ _____   _____

$ _____   _____

$ _____   _____

$ _____   _____

CRUISE SAVINGS

DEPOSIT TRACKER

AMOUNT DEPOSITED: **DATE DEPOSITED:**

$ _____

$ _____

$ _____

$ _____

$ _____

$ _____

$ _____

$ _____

$ _____

$ _____

$ _____

$ _____

$ _____

ALL ABOARD!

PRE-CRUISE TO DO LIST & CHECKLIST

1 MONTH BEFORE

2 WEEKS BEFORE

1 WEEK BEFORE

2 DAYS BEFORE

24 HOURS BEFORE

DAY OF TRAVEL

FLIGHT INFORMATION

DATE:	DESTINATION:

AIRLINE:	
BOOKING NUMBER:	
DEPARTURE DATE:	
BOARDING TIME:	
GATE NUMBER:	
SEAT NUMBER:	
ARRIVAL / LANDING TIME:	

DATE:	DESTINATION:

AIRLINE:	
BOOKING NUMBER:	
DEPARTURE DATE:	
BOARDING TIME:	
GATE NUMBER:	
SEAT NUMBER:	
ARRIVAL / LANDING TIME:	

CRUISE PACKING CHECKLIST

CLOTHING	✓	ESSENTIALS	✓

CRUISE PACKING CHECKLIST

CLOTHING FOR HER	✓	CLOTHING FOR HIM	✓

ESSENTIALS	✓	FOR THE JOURNEY	✓
		IMPORTANT DOCUMENTS	✓

SAMPLE CRUISE PACKING CHECKLIST

CLOTHING FOR HER	✓	CLOTHING FOR HIM	✓
T-Shirts &, Tank Tops & Blouses		T-Shirts & Tank Tops	
Sundresses		Shorts	
Flip Flops, Sandals & Heels		Swim Wear	
Shorts & Pants		Jeans, Khakis	
Swimsuit & Cover Up		Formal Attire (dress shirt, shoes, etc.)	
T-Shirts &, Tank Tops & Blouses		Belt	
Aqua/Swimming Shoes		Tie	
Bras, Panties & Socks		Sandals / Sneakers	
Sunhat		Visor, Baseball Cap	
Sunglasses		T-Shirts &, Tank Tops & Blouses	
Formal Attire		Sunglasses	
Jewelry		Socks & Underwear	

ESSENTIALS	✓	FOR THE JOURNEY	✓
Lanyard		Carry On Bag	
Suntan Lotion		Cash / Local Currency	
Medication (motion sickness, etc.)		Credit Cards	
Travel Mug / Water Bottle		Phone Charger	
		Backpack	

		IMPORTANT DOCUMENTS	✓
		Passport & ID	
		Cruise Documents & Boarding Pass	
		Flight Information	

CRUISE ITINERARY

Monday

Tuesday

Wednesday

Thursday

Friday

Saturday

Sunday

CRUISE DETAILS

NOTES

TO DO:

CRUISE DETAILS & REMINDERS:

CRUISING TO DO LIST

CRUISE EXCURSION PLANNER

ACTIVITY / EXCURSION OVERVIEW:

EST COST OF EXCURSION:

INCLUSIONS:	✓	**EXCLUSIONS:**	✓
FOOD & DRINK:	☐		☐
TRANSPORTATION:	☐		☐
GRATUITY:	☐		☐

ACTUAL COST:

IMPORTANT INFORMATION:

CONTACT: _____ PHONE #: _____

MEET UP TIME: _____ WHAT TO BRING: _____

ADDRESS: _____

CRUISE EXCURSION PLANNER

ACTIVITY / EXCURSION OVERVIEW:

EST COST OF EXCURSION: _____

INCLUSIONS:	✓	**EXCLUSIONS:**	✓
FOOD & DRINK:	☐		☐
TRANSPORTATION:	☐		☐
GRATUITY:	☐		☐

ACTUAL COST:

IMPORTANT INFORMATION:

CONTACT: _____   PHONE #: _____

MEET UP TIME: _____   WHAT TO BRING: _____

ADDRESS: _____

_____

CRUISE EXCURSION PLANNER

ACTIVITY / EXCURSION OVERVIEW:

EST COST OF EXCURSION:

INCLUSIONS:	✓	EXCLUSIONS:	✓
FOOD & DRINK:	☐		☐
TRANSPORTATION:	☐		☐
GRATUITY:	☐		☐

ACTUAL COST:

IMPORTANT INFORMATION:

CONTACT: _____ PHONE #: _____

MEET UP TIME: _____ WHAT TO BRING: _____

ADDRESS: _____

CRUISE EXCURSION PLANNER

ACTIVITY / EXCURSION OVERVIEW:

EST COST OF EXCURSION:

INCLUSIONS:	✓	**EXCLUSIONS:**	✓
FOOD & DRINK:	☐		☐
TRANSPORTATION:	☐		☐
GRATUITY:	☐		☐

ACTUAL COST:

IMPORTANT INFORMATION:

CONTACT: _____ PHONE #: _____

MEET UP TIME: _____ WHAT TO BRING: _____

ADDRESS: _____

CRUISE PORT PLANNER

DESTINATION:	DATE:

THINGS TO DO / SEE:

☐
☐
☐
☐
☐
☐
☐

WHERE TO EAT:

☐
☐
☐
☐
☐
☐
☐

TRANSPORTATION DETAILS:

☐
☐
☐
☐
☐

OTHER INFORMATION:

☐
☐
☐
☐
☐

RETURN TO SHIP BY:

CRUISE PORT PLANNER

DESTINATION: DATE:

THINGS TO DO / SEE:

☐
☐
☐
☐
☐
☐
☐

WHERE TO EAT:

☐
☐
☐
☐
☐
☐
☐

TRANSPORTATION DETAILS:

☐
☐
☐
☐
☐

OTHER INFORMATION:

☐
☐
☐
☐
☐

RETURN TO SHIP BY:

CRUISE PORT PLANNER

DESTINATION:	DATE:

THINGS TO DO / SEE:

WHERE TO EAT:

TRANSPORTATION DETAILS:

OTHER INFORMATION:

RETURN TO SHIP BY:

CRUISE PORT PLANNER

DESTINATION:	DATE:

THINGS TO DO / SEE:

☐
☐
☐
☐
☐
☐
☐

WHERE TO EAT:

☐
☐
☐
☐
☐
☐
☐

TRANSPORTATION DETAILS:

☐
☐
☐
☐
☐

OTHER INFORMATION:

☐
☐
☐
☐
☐

RETURN TO SHIP BY:

CRUISE PORT PLANNER

DESTINATION: DATE:

THINGS TO DO / SEE:

WHERE TO EAT:

TRANSPORTATION DETAILS:

OTHER INFORMATION:

RETURN TO SHIP BY:

CRUISE PLANNER

WEEK OF:

MONDAY	TUESDAY	WEDNESDAY	THURSDAY

TO DO	TO DO	TO DO	TO DO

MEALS	MEALS	MEALS	MEALS

FRIDAY	SATURDAY	SUNDAY	NOTES

TO DO	TO DO	TO DO	

MEALS	MEALS	MEALS	MEALS

CRUISE ACTIVITIES

ACTIVITY PLANNER:

	M	T	W	T	F	S	S
	○	○	○	○	○	○	○
	○	○	○	○	○	○	○
	○	○	○	○	○	○	○
	○	○	○	○	○	○	○
	○	○	○	○	○	○	○
	○	○	○	○	○	○	○
	○	○	○	○	○	○	○
	○	○	○	○	○	○	○
	○	○	○	○	○	○	○
	○	○	○	○	○	○	○
	○	○	○	○	○	○	○
	○	○	○	○	○	○	○
	○	○	○	○	○	○	○
	○	○	○	○	○	○	○
	○	○	○	○	○	○	○

DAILY ACTIVITY PLANNER

DAILY ITINERARY

ACTIVITY: _____

TIME: _____

LOCATION: _____

WEATHER: ☀ ⛅ 🌦 ☁ ⛈

MEAL PLANNER

TOP ACTIVITIES

TIME:	SCHEDULE:

DAILY EXPENSES

_____ _____

_____ _____

_____ _____

_____ _____

TOTAL COST: [   ]

NOTES:

DAILY ACTIVITY PLANNER

DAILY ITINERARY

ACTIVITY:

TIME:

LOCATION:

WEATHER:

MEAL PLANNER

DAILY EXPENSES

TOTAL COST:

TOP ACTIVITIES

TIME:	SCHEDULE:

NOTES:

DAILY ACTIVITY PLANNER

DAILY ITINERARY

ACTIVITY: _____

TIME: _____

LOCATION: _____

WEATHER: ☀ ⛅ 🌦 ☁ ⛈

MEAL PLANNER

DAILY EXPENSES

_____ _____

_____ _____

_____ _____

_____ _____

_____

TOTAL COST: [   ]

TOP ACTIVITIES

TIME:	SCHEDULE:

NOTES:

DAILY ACTIVITY PLANNER

DAILY ITINERARY

ACTIVITY: ....

TIME: ....

LOCATION: ....

WEATHER: ☀ ⛅ 🌦 ☁ ⛈

MEAL PLANNER

TOP ACTIVITIES

TIME:	SCHEDULE:

DAILY EXPENSES

TOTAL COST: [   ]

NOTES:

DAILY ACTIVITY PLANNER

DAILY ITINERARY

ACTIVITY: ....

TIME: ....

LOCATION: ....

WEATHER: ☀ ⛅ 🌦 ☁ ⛈

MEAL PLANNER

TOP ACTIVITIES

TIME:	SCHEDULE:

DAILY EXPENSES

....

....

....

....

....

TOTAL COST: [   ]

NOTES:

DAILY ACTIVITY PLANNER

DAILY ITINERARY

ACTIVITY: _____

TIME: _____

LOCATION: _____

WEATHER: ☀️ ⛅ 🌦️ ☁️ ⛈️

MEAL PLANNER

DAILY EXPENSES

_____

_____ _____

_____ _____

_____ _____

_____ _____

TOTAL COST: [_____]

TOP ACTIVITIES

TIME:	SCHEDULE:

NOTES:

DAILY ACTIVITY PLANNER

DAILY ITINERARY

ACTIVITY: ....

TIME: ....

LOCATION: ....

WEATHER: ☀ ⛅ 🌦 ☁ ⛈

MEAL PLANNER

TOP ACTIVITIES

TIME:	SCHEDULE:

DAILY EXPENSES

TOTAL COST:

NOTES:

MY CRUISE JOURNAL

DATE:

What I Did Today:

Highlight of the Day:

Thoughts & Reflections:

MY CRUISE JOURNAL

DATE:

What I Did Today:

Highlight of the Day:

Thoughts & Reflections:

MY CRUISE JOURNAL

DATE:

What I Did Today:

Highlight of the Day:

Thoughts & Reflections:

MY CRUISE JOURNAL

DATE:

What I Did Today:

Highlight of the Day:

Thoughts & Reflections:

MY CRUISE JOURNAL

DATE:

What I Did Today:

Highlight of the Day:

Thoughts & Reflections:

MY CRUISE JOURNAL

DATE:

What I Did Today:

Highlight of the Day:

Thoughts & Reflections:

MY CRUISE JOURNAL

DATE:

What I Did Today:

Highlight of the Day:

Thoughts & Reflections:

CRUISE FRIENDS

FRIENDS ARE FOREVER

NAME:

PHONE NUMBER:

ADDRESS:

CABIN #:

FRIENDS ARE FOREVER

NAME:

PHONE NUMBER:

ADDRESS:

CABIN #:

FRIENDS ARE FOREVER

NAME:

PHONE NUMBER:

ADDRESS:

CABIN #:

FRIENDS ARE FOREVER

NAME:

PHONE NUMBER:

ADDRESS:

CABIN #:

There's Nothing Like Cruising Life!

CRUISE SAVINGS

WE'RE SAVING FOR: _____

AMOUNT NEEDED: _____

OUR GOAL DATE:

$

DEPOSIT TRACKER

AMOUNT DEPOSITED: **DATE DEPOSITED:**

$ _____   _____

$ _____   _____

$ _____   _____

$ _____   _____

$ _____   _____

$ _____   _____

$ _____   _____

$ _____   _____

$ _____   _____

$ _____   _____

CRUISE SAVINGS

DEPOSIT TRACKER

AMOUNT DEPOSITED: **DATE DEPOSITED:**

$ _____   _____

$ _____   _____

$ _____   _____

$ _____   _____

$ _____   _____

$ _____   _____

$ _____   _____

$ _____   _____

$ _____   _____

$ _____   _____

$ _____   _____

$ _____   _____

$ _____   _____

$ _____   _____

ALL ABOARD!

PRE-CRUISE TO DO LIST & CHECKLIST

1 MONTH BEFORE

- [ ] ....
- [ ] ....
- [ ] ....
- [ ] ....
- [ ] ....

2 WEEKS BEFORE

- [ ] ....
- [ ] ....
- [ ] ....
- [ ] ....
- [ ] ....

1 WEEK BEFORE

- [ ] ....
- [ ] ....
- [ ] ....
- [ ] ....
- [ ] ....

2 DAYS BEFORE

- [ ] ....
- [ ] ....
- [ ] ....
- [ ] ....
- [ ] ....

24 HOURS BEFORE

- [ ] ....
- [ ] ....
- [ ] ....
- [ ] ....
- [ ] ....

DAY OF TRAVEL

- [ ] ....
- [ ] ....
- [ ] ....
- [ ] ....
- [ ] ....

FLIGHT INFORMATION

DATE:	DESTINATION:

AIRLINE:	
BOOKING NUMBER:	
DEPARTURE DATE:	
BOARDING TIME:	
GATE NUMBER:	
SEAT NUMBER:	
ARRIVAL / LANDING TIME:	

DATE:	DESTINATION:

AIRLINE:	
BOOKING NUMBER:	
DEPARTURE DATE:	
BOARDING TIME:	
GATE NUMBER:	
SEAT NUMBER:	
ARRIVAL / LANDING TIME:	

CRUISE PACKING CHECKLIST

CLOTHING	✓	ESSENTIALS	✓

CRUISE PACKING CHECKLIST

CLOTHING FOR HER	✓	CLOTHING FOR HIM	✓

ESSENTIALS	✓	FOR THE JOURNEY	✓
		IMPORTANT DOCUMENTS	✓

SAMPLE CRUISE PACKING CHECKLIST

CLOTHING FOR HER	✓	CLOTHING FOR HIM	✓
T-Shirts &, Tank Tops & Blouses		T-Shirts & Tank Tops	
Sundresses		Shorts	
Flip Flops, Sandals & Heels		Swim Wear	
Shorts & Pants		Jeans, Khakis	
Swimsuit & Cover Up		Formal Attire (dress shirt, shoes, etc.)	
T-Shirts &, Tank Tops & Blouses		Belt	
Aqua/Swimming Shoes		Tie	
Bras, Panties & Socks		Sandals / Sneakers	
Sunhat		Visor, Baseball Cap	
Sunglasses		T-Shirts &, Tank Tops & Blouses	
Formal Attire		Sunglasses	
Jewelry		Socks & Underwear	

ESSENTIALS	✓	FOR THE JOURNEY	✓
Lanyard		Carry On Bag	
Suntan Lotion		Cash / Local Currency	
Medication (motion sickness, etc.)		Credit Cards	
Travel Mug / Water Bottle		Phone Charger	
		Backpack	
		IMPORTANT DOCUMENTS	✓
		Passport & ID	
		Cruise Documents & Boarding Pass	
		Flight Information	

CRUISE ITINERARY

Monday

Tuesday

Wednesday

Thursday

Friday

Saturday

Sunday

CRUISE DETAILS

NOTES

TO DO:

CRUISE DETAILS & REMINDERS:

CRUISING TO DO LIST

CRUISE EXCURSION PLANNER

ACTIVITY / EXCURSION OVERVIEW:

EST COST OF EXCURSION: _____

INCLUSIONS: ✓

FOOD & DRINK: ☐

TRANSPORTATION: ☐

GRATUITY: ☐

EXCLUSIONS: ✓

☐

☐

☐

ACTUAL COST:

IMPORTANT INFORMATION:

CONTACT: _____ PHONE #: _____

MEET UP TIME: _____ WHAT TO BRING: _____

ADDRESS: _____

CRUISE EXCURSION PLANNER

ACTIVITY / EXCURSION OVERVIEW:

EST COST OF EXCURSION: _____

INCLUSIONS:	✓	**EXCLUSIONS:**	✓
FOOD & DRINK:	☐		☐
TRANSPORTATION:	☐		☐
GRATUITY:	☐		☐

ACTUAL COST:

IMPORTANT INFORMATION:

CONTACT: _____   PHONE #: _____

MEET UP TIME: _____   WHAT TO BRING: _____

ADDRESS: _____

CRUISE EXCURSION PLANNER

ACTIVITY / EXCURSION OVERVIEW:

EST COST OF EXCURSION: _____

INCLUSIONS:	✓	**EXCLUSIONS:**	✓
FOOD & DRINK:	☐		☐
TRANSPORTATION:	☐		☐
GRATUITY:	☐		☐

ACTUAL COST:

IMPORTANT INFORMATION:

CONTACT: _____ PHONE #: _____

MEET UP TIME: _____ WHAT TO BRING: _____

ADDRESS: _____

CRUISE EXCURSION PLANNER

ACTIVITY / EXCURSION OVERVIEW:

EST COST OF EXCURSION:

INCLUSIONS:	✓	EXCLUSIONS:	✓
FOOD & DRINK:	☐		☐
TRANSPORTATION:	☐		☐
GRATUITY:	☐		☐

ACTUAL COST:

IMPORTANT INFORMATION:

CONTACT: PHONE #:

MEET UP TIME: WHAT TO BRING:

ADDRESS:

CRUISE PORT PLANNER

DESTINATION: | DATE:

THINGS TO DO / SEE:

WHERE TO EAT:

TRANSPORTATION DETAILS:

OTHER INFORMATION:

RETURN TO SHIP BY:

CRUISE PORT PLANNER

DESTINATION: **DATE:**

THINGS TO DO / SEE:

- ☐
- ☐
- ☐
- ☐
- ☐
- ☐
- ☐

WHERE TO EAT:

- ☐
- ☐
- ☐
- ☐
- ☐
- ☐

TRANSPORTATION DETAILS:

- ☐
- ☐
- ☐
- ☐
- ☐

OTHER INFORMATION:

- ☐
- ☐
- ☐
- ☐
- ☐

RETURN TO SHIP BY:

CRUISE PORT PLANNER

DESTINATION: DATE:

THINGS TO DO / SEE:

☐
☐
☐
☐
☐
☐
☐

WHERE TO EAT:

☐
☐
☐
☐
☐
☐
☐

TRANSPORTATION DETAILS:

☐
☐
☐
☐
☐

OTHER INFORMATION:

☐
☐
☐
☐
☐

RETURN TO SHIP BY:

CRUISE PORT PLANNER

DESTINATION: DATE:

THINGS TO DO / SEE:

☐
☐
☐
☐
☐
☐
☐

WHERE TO EAT:

☐
☐
☐
☐
☐
☐
☐

TRANSPORTATION DETAILS:

☐
☐
☐
☐
☐

OTHER INFORMATION:

☐
☐
☐
☐
☐

RETURN TO SHIP BY:

CRUISE PORT PLANNER

DESTINATION: DATE:

THINGS TO DO / SEE:

WHERE TO EAT:

TRANSPORTATION DETAILS:

OTHER INFORMATION:

RETURN TO SHIP BY:

CRUISE PLANNER

WEEK OF:

MONDAY	TUESDAY	WEDNESDAY	THURSDAY
TO DO	TO DO	TO DO	TO DO
MEALS	MEALS	MEALS	MEALS

FRIDAY	SATURDAY	SUNDAY	NOTES
TO DO	TO DO	TO DO	
MEALS	MEALS	MEALS	MEALS

CRUISE ACTIVITIES

ACTIVITY PLANNER:

	M	T	W	T	F	S	S
	○	○	○	○	○	○	○
	○	○	○	○	○	○	○
	○	○	○	○	○	○	○
	○	○	○	○	○	○	○
	○	○	○	○	○	○	○
	○	○	○	○	○	○	○
	○	○	○	○	○	○	○
	○	○	○	○	○	○	○
	○	○	○	○	○	○	○
	○	○	○	○	○	○	○
	○	○	○	○	○	○	○
	○	○	○	○	○	○	○
	○	○	○	○	○	○	○
	○	○	○	○	○	○	○
	○	○	○	○	○	○	○

DAILY ACTIVITY PLANNER

DAILY ITINERARY

ACTIVITY: ....

TIME: ....

LOCATION: ....

WEATHER: ☀ ⛅ 🌦 ☁ ⛈

MEAL PLANNER

DAILY EXPENSES

TOTAL COST:

TOP ACTIVITIES

TIME:	SCHEDULE:

NOTES:

DAILY ACTIVITY PLANNER

DAILY ITINERARY

ACTIVITY: _____

TIME: _____

LOCATION: _____

WEATHER: ☀ ⛅ 🌦 ☁ ⛈

MEAL PLANNER

TOP ACTIVITIES

TIME:	SCHEDULE:

DAILY EXPENSES

_____   _____

_____   _____

_____   _____

_____   _____

TOTAL COST: [_____]

NOTES:

DAILY ACTIVITY PLANNER

DAILY ITINERARY

ACTIVITY: _____

TIME: _____

LOCATION: _____

WEATHER: ☀ ⛅ 🌦 ☁ ⛈

MEAL PLANNER

TOP ACTIVITIES

TIME:	SCHEDULE:

DAILY EXPENSES

_____ _____

_____ _____

_____ _____

_____ _____

TOTAL COST: _____

NOTES:

DAILY ACTIVITY PLANNER

DAILY ITINERARY

ACTIVITY: ....

TIME: ....

LOCATION: ....

WEATHER:

MEAL PLANNER

DAILY EXPENSES

TOTAL COST:

TOP ACTIVITIES

TIME: SCHEDULE:

NOTES:

DAILY ACTIVITY PLANNER

DAILY ITINERARY

ACTIVITY: ....

TIME: ....

LOCATION: ....

WEATHER: ☀ ⛅ 🌦 ☁ ⛈

MEAL PLANNER

TOP ACTIVITIES

TIME:	SCHEDULE:

DAILY EXPENSES

TOTAL COST: [   ]

NOTES:

DAILY ACTIVITY PLANNER

DAILY ITINERARY

ACTIVITY: ....

TIME: ....

LOCATION: ....

WEATHER: ☀ ⛅ 🌦 ☁ ⛈

MEAL PLANNER

TOP ACTIVITIES

TIME:	SCHEDULE:

DAILY EXPENSES

TOTAL COST: [   ]

NOTES:

DAILY ACTIVITY PLANNER

DAILY ITINERARY

ACTIVITY: ....

TIME: ....

LOCATION: ....

WEATHER:

TOP ACTIVITIES

MEAL PLANNER

TIME:	SCHEDULE:

DAILY EXPENSES

TOTAL COST:

NOTES:

MY CRUISE JOURNAL

DATE:

What I Did Today:

Highlight of the Day:

Thoughts & Reflections:

MY CRUISE JOURNAL

DATE:

What I Did Today:

Highlight of the Day:

Thoughts & Reflections:

MY CRUISE JOURNAL

DATE:

What I Did Today:

Highlight of the Day:

Thoughts & Reflections:

MY CRUISE JOURNAL

DATE:

What I Did Today:

Highlight of the Day:

Thoughts & Reflections:

MY CRUISE JOURNAL

DATE:

What I Did Today:

Highlight of the Day:

Thoughts & Reflections:

MY CRUISE JOURNAL

DATE:

What I Did Today:

Highlight of the Day:

Thoughts & Reflections:

MY CRUISE JOURNAL

DATE:

What I Did Today:

Highlight of the Day:

Thoughts & Reflections:

CRUISE FRIENDS

FRIENDS ARE FOREVER

NAME:

PHONE NUMBER:

ADDRESS:

CABIN #:

FRIENDS ARE FOREVER

NAME:

PHONE NUMBER:

ADDRESS:

CABIN #:

FRIENDS ARE FOREVER

NAME:

PHONE NUMBER:

ADDRESS:

CABIN #:

FRIENDS ARE FOREVER

NAME:

PHONE NUMBER:

ADDRESS:

CABIN #:

There's Nothing Like Cruising Life!

CRUISE SAVINGS

WE'RE SAVING FOR:

AMOUNT NEEDED:

OUR GOAL DATE:

$

DEPOSIT TRACKER

AMOUNT DEPOSITED: **DATE DEPOSITED:**

$

$

$

$

$

$

$

$

$

$

CRUISE SAVINGS

DEPOSIT TRACKER

AMOUNT DEPOSITED: **DATE DEPOSITED:**

$ _____   _____

$ _____   _____

$ _____   _____

$ _____   _____

$ _____   _____

$ _____   _____

$ _____   _____

$ _____   _____

$ _____   _____

$ _____   _____

$ _____   _____

$ _____   _____

$ _____   _____

$ _____   _____

ALL ABOARD!

PRE-CRUISE TO DO LIST & CHECKLIST

1 MONTH BEFORE

2 WEEKS BEFORE

1 WEEK BEFORE

2 DAYS BEFORE

24 HOURS BEFORE

DAY OF TRAVEL

FLIGHT INFORMATION

DATE:	DESTINATION:

AIRLINE:	
BOOKING NUMBER:	
DEPARTURE DATE:	
BOARDING TIME:	
GATE NUMBER:	
SEAT NUMBER:	
ARRIVAL / LANDING TIME:	

DATE:	DESTINATION:

AIRLINE:	
BOOKING NUMBER:	
DEPARTURE DATE:	
BOARDING TIME:	
GATE NUMBER:	
SEAT NUMBER:	
ARRIVAL / LANDING TIME:	

CRUISE PACKING CHECKLIST

CLOTHING	✓	ESSENTIALS	✓

CRUISE PACKING CHECKLIST

CLOTHING FOR HER	✓	CLOTHING FOR HIM	✓

ESSENTIALS	✓	FOR THE JOURNEY	✓
		IMPORTANT DOCUMENTS	✓

SAMPLE CRUISE PACKING CHECKLIST

CLOTHING FOR HER	✓	CLOTHING FOR HIM	✓
T-Shirts &, Tank Tops & Blouses		T-Shirts & Tank Tops	
Sundresses		Shorts	
Flip Flops, Sandals & Heels		Swim Wear	
Shorts & Pants		Jeans, Khakis	
Swimsuit & Cover Up		Formal Attire (dress shirt, shoes, etc.)	
T-Shirts &, Tank Tops & Blouses		Belt	
Aqua/Swimming Shoes		Tie	
Bras, Panties & Socks		Sandals / Sneakers	
Sunhat		Visor, Baseball Cap	
Sunglasses		T-Shirts &, Tank Tops & Blouses	
Formal Attire		Sunglasses	
Jewelry		Socks & Underwear	

ESSENTIALS	✓	FOR THE JOURNEY	✓
Lanyard		Carry On Bag	
Suntan Lotion		Cash / Local Currency	
Medication (motion sickness, etc.)		Credit Cards	
Travel Mug / Water Bottle		Phone Charger	
		Backpack	
		IMPORTANT DOCUMENTS	✓
		Passport & ID	
		Cruise Documents & Boarding Pass	
		Flight Information	

CRUISE ITINERARY

Monday

Tuesday

Wednesday

Thursday

Friday

Saturday

Sunday

CRUISE DETAILS

NOTES

TO DO:

CRUISE DETAILS & REMINDERS:

CRUISING TO DO LIST

CRUISE EXCURSION PLANNER

ACTIVITY / EXCURSION OVERVIEW:

EST COST OF EXCURSION:

INCLUSIONS:	✓	**EXCLUSIONS:**	✓
FOOD & DRINK:	☐		☐
TRANSPORTATION:	☐		☐
GRATUITY:	☐		☐

ACTUAL COST:

IMPORTANT INFORMATION:

CONTACT: _____ PHONE #: _____

MEET UP TIME: _____ WHAT TO BRING: _____

ADDRESS:

CRUISE EXCURSION PLANNER

ACTIVITY / EXCURSION OVERVIEW:

EST COST OF EXCURSION: _____

INCLUSIONS:	✓	**EXCLUSIONS:**	✓
FOOD & DRINK:	☐	_____	☐
TRANSPORTATION:	☐	_____	☐
GRATUITY:	☐	_____	☐

ACTUAL COST: _____

IMPORTANT INFORMATION:

CONTACT: _____   PHONE #: _____

MEET UP TIME: _____   WHAT TO BRING: _____

ADDRESS: _____

_____   _____

CRUISE EXCURSION PLANNER

ACTIVITY / EXCURSION OVERVIEW:

EST COST OF EXCURSION:

INCLUSIONS:	✓	**EXCLUSIONS:**	✓
FOOD & DRINK:	☐		☐
TRANSPORTATION:	☐		☐
GRATUITY:	☐		☐

ACTUAL COST:

IMPORTANT INFORMATION:

CONTACT: _____ PHONE #: _____

MEET UP TIME: _____ WHAT TO BRING: _____

ADDRESS: _____

CRUISE EXCURSION PLANNER

ACTIVITY / EXCURSION OVERVIEW:

EST COST OF EXCURSION: _____

INCLUSIONS:	✓		**EXCLUSIONS:**	✓
FOOD & DRINK:	☐		☐
TRANSPORTATION:	☐		☐
GRATUITY:	☐		☐

ACTUAL COST: _____

IMPORTANT INFORMATION:

CONTACT: _____ PHONE #: _____

MEET UP TIME: _____ WHAT TO BRING: _____

ADDRESS: _____

CRUISE PORT PLANNER

DESTINATION: DATE:

THINGS TO DO / SEE:

WHERE TO EAT:

TRANSPORTATION DETAILS:

OTHER INFORMATION:

RETURN TO SHIP BY:

CRUISE PORT PLANNER

DESTINATION: DATE:

THINGS TO DO / SEE:

WHERE TO EAT:

TRANSPORTATION DETAILS:

OTHER INFORMATION:

RETURN TO SHIP BY:

CRUISE PORT PLANNER

DESTINATION: DATE:

THINGS TO DO / SEE:

WHERE TO EAT:

TRANSPORTATION DETAILS:

OTHER INFORMATION:

RETURN TO SHIP BY:

CRUISE PORT PLANNER

DESTINATION: DATE:

THINGS TO DO / SEE:

☐
☐
☐
☐
☐
☐
☐

WHERE TO EAT:

☐
☐
☐
☐
☐
☐
☐

TRANSPORTATION DETAILS:

☐
☐
☐
☐
☐

OTHER INFORMATION:

☐
☐
☐
☐
☐

RETURN TO SHIP BY:

CRUISE PORT PLANNER

DESTINATION:	DATE:

THINGS TO DO / SEE:

WHERE TO EAT:

TRANSPORTATION DETAILS:

OTHER INFORMATION:

RETURN TO SHIP BY:

CRUISE PLANNER

WEEK OF:

MONDAY	TUESDAY	WEDNESDAY	THURSDAY
TO DO	TO DO	TO DO	TO DO
MEALS	MEALS	MEALS	MEALS

FRIDAY	SATURDAY	SUNDAY	NOTES
TO DO	TO DO	TO DO	
MEALS	MEALS	MEALS	MEALS

CRUISE ACTIVITIES

ACTIVITY PLANNER:

	M	T	W	T	F	S	S
	○	○	○	○	○	○	○
	○	○	○	○	○	○	○
	○	○	○	○	○	○	○
	○	○	○	○	○	○	○
	○	○	○	○	○	○	○
	○	○	○	○	○	○	○
	○	○	○	○	○	○	○
	○	○	○	○	○	○	○
	○	○	○	○	○	○	○
	○	○	○	○	○	○	○
	○	○	○	○	○	○	○
	○	○	○	○	○	○	○
	○	○	○	○	○	○	○
	○	○	○	○	○	○	○
	○	○	○	○	○	○	○

DAILY ACTIVITY PLANNER

DAILY ITINERARY

ACTIVITY: ....

TIME: ....

LOCATION: ....

WEATHER: ☀ ⛅ 🌦 ☁ ⛈

MEAL PLANNER

DAILY EXPENSES

TOTAL COST:

TOP ACTIVITIES

TIME: SCHEDULE:

NOTES:

DAILY ACTIVITY PLANNER

DAILY ITINERARY

ACTIVITY: ....

TIME: ....

LOCATION: ....

WEATHER: ☀ ⛅ 🌦 ☁ ⛈

MEAL PLANNER

DAILY EXPENSES

TOTAL COST: [   ]

TOP ACTIVITIES

TIME:	SCHEDULE:

NOTES:

DAILY ACTIVITY PLANNER

DAILY ITINERARY

ACTIVITY: ....

TIME: ....

LOCATION: ....

WEATHER:

MEAL PLANNER

DAILY EXPENSES

TOTAL COST:

TOP ACTIVITIES

TIME: | SCHEDULE:

NOTES:

DAILY ACTIVITY PLANNER

DAILY ITINERARY

ACTIVITY: ....

TIME: ....

LOCATION: ....

WEATHER: ☀ ⛅ 🌦 ☁ ⛈

MEAL PLANNER

DAILY EXPENSES

TOTAL COST: [ ]

TOP ACTIVITIES

TIME:	SCHEDULE:

NOTES:

DAILY ACTIVITY PLANNER

DAILY ITINERARY

ACTIVITY: ....

TIME: ....

LOCATION: ....

WEATHER: ☀ ⛅ 🌧 ☁ ⛈

MEAL PLANNER

DAILY EXPENSES

....

....

....

....

....

TOTAL COST:

TOP ACTIVITIES

TIME:	SCHEDULE:

NOTES:

DAILY ACTIVITY PLANNER

DAILY ITINERARY

ACTIVITY: _____

TIME: _____

LOCATION: _____

WEATHER:

MEAL PLANNER

DAILY EXPENSES

_____ _____

_____ _____

_____ _____

_____ _____

_____ _____

TOTAL COST: [   ]

TOP ACTIVITIES

TIME:	SCHEDULE:

NOTES:

DAILY ACTIVITY PLANNER

DAILY ITINERARY

ACTIVITY: ....

TIME: ....

LOCATION: ....

WEATHER:

TOP ACTIVITIES

MEAL PLANNER

TIME: SCHEDULE:

DAILY EXPENSES

TOTAL COST:

NOTES:

MY CRUISE JOURNAL

DATE:

What I Did Today:

Highlight of the Day:

Thoughts & Reflections:

MY CRUISE JOURNAL

DATE:

What I Did Today:

Highlight of the Day:

Thoughts & Reflections:

MY CRUISE JOURNAL

DATE:

What I Did Today:

Highlight of the Day:

Thoughts & Reflections:

MY CRUISE JOURNAL

DATE:

What I Did Today:

Highlight of the Day:

Thoughts & Reflections:

MY CRUISE JOURNAL

DATE:

What I Did Today:

Highlight of the Day:

Thoughts & Reflections:

MY CRUISE JOURNAL

DATE:

What I Did Today:

Highlight of the Day:

Thoughts & Reflections:

MY CRUISE JOURNAL

DATE:

What I Did Today:

Highlight of the Day:

Thoughts & Reflections:

CRUISE FRIENDS

FRIENDS ARE FOREVER

NAME:

PHONE NUMBER:

ADDRESS:

CABIN #:

FRIENDS ARE FOREVER

NAME:

PHONE NUMBER:

ADDRESS:

CABIN #:

FRIENDS ARE FOREVER

NAME:

PHONE NUMBER:

ADDRESS:

CABIN #:

FRIENDS ARE FOREVER

NAME:

PHONE NUMBER:

ADDRESS:

CABIN #:

There's Nothing Like Cruising Life!

Made in the USA
Monee, IL
14 September 2023

42743042R00083